W9-CII-931

COMPASSION

Caring for others is at the center of what makes us human.

THE VALUES LIBRARY

COMPASSION

Alice Margulies

THE ROSEN PUBLISHING GROUP, INC.

NEW YORK

Published in 1990 by The Rosen Publishing Group, Inc.
29 East 21st Street, New York, NY 10010.

First Edition
Copyright 1990 by The Rosen Publishing Group, Inc.

Printed in Canada

Library of Congress Cataloging-in-Publication Data

Margulies, Alice.
    Compassion / Alice Margulies.
    (The Values library)
    Includes bibliographical references.
    Summary: Discusses the levels, significance, and effects of
compassion and how it relates to science, the great religions, and
conduct in a world of daily violence and tragedy.
    ISBN 0-8239-1108-X
    1. Caring—Juvenile literature. 2. Sympathy—Juvenile literature.
3. Youth—Conduct of life. [1. Caring. 2. Sympathy. 3. Conduct
of life.] I. Title. II. Series.
BJ1475.M37   1989   89-27527
177'.7—dc20   CIP
                                                          AC

CONTENTS

1

THE SIX O'CLOCK NEWS

SIX O'CLOCK. Time for the network news. People everywhere are watching it.

A young married couple in the city are watching the news while they eat dinner. In the suburbs, teenagers are watching it upstairs in their rooms, just to put off doing their homework. Drug dealers measuring out cocaine are watching it. Off-duty cops are watching it. People in duplexes in luxury apartment buildings are watching it. Homeless families in tiny welfare hotel rooms are watching it.

All over the state, people who will never meet each other are watching the same network news.

The anchorman announces the major stories. What kind of a day has it been for the people in the news? Not very good, for most of them. But then, every day is a bad day for somebody, somewhere.

"An estimated 10,000 Mexico City residents died in an earthquake yesterday. Emergency workers hunt for survivors, guided by the cries coming up through the rubble...."

"Sally Anne Kelly, the 11-year-old reported missing from her New Jersey home two weeks ago, was found dead in a trash can by sanitation workers this morning. Police said she had apparently been raped and beaten to death...."

"International relief agencies called the Ethiopian famine the worst of the decade...."

"Two homeless women froze to death in Central Park last night...."

And, of course, the newscast reported on the "human interest" story of the day:

"Koko the chimp returns, safe, to the Wilmington zoo."

No two people respond to the news in exactly the same way.

The teenagers discuss the news upstairs in their room.

"Wow, what a day!"

"I'm sure glad Koko's back."

"Yeah, that's a relief."

"That chimp had me worried."

The woman eating dinner says, "Oh God, that poor child's family. At least the suspense is over for them. My God, can you imagine how that feels?"

"What?" says the husband.

Reporters are often caught between the demands of their job and their compassionate feelings.

"Sally Anne Kelly. The missing one? They found her body."

"Really — that's too bad. Where's the salt?"

There are all kinds of reactions, everywhere. It's impossible to predict who will react in what way. Some people are interested, others don't seem to care. Some people get excited, some don't seem to get involved. There are so many reactions you can have when you learn about somebody else's trouble.

Meanwhile, reporters are following up the Sally Anne Kelly story. Sally Anne's mother is on the way back from identifying the body.

News people, camera people and sound people close in on her. For weeks she's been talking to the news people. They were helping her. Spreading the word was her best chance to find her child. Now she doesn't want to answer any more questions. "Please, no comment," she keeps telling them. "I have nothing to say." Finally she screams at the reporters: "Don't you see—*it's over!* It's over. Why don't you leave me alone? Don't you have any shame? Don't you have any pity? Don't you have any *compassion?*"

The reporters are human, so most of them *are* ashamed. Most of them do feel compassion. Some of them think: I wonder if reporting this kind of thing every day is making me hard inside?

They forget that *we watch it* every day. Does it make *us* hard inside too? And why is it, anyway, that we like to watch such things? The news people wouldn't go after interviews with mothers whose children were murdered if we weren't interested. Sometimes people ask, "Why don't you report more *good* news?" But that's not the news that people buy. We seem to be interested in other people's

The homeless are now part
of our everyday lives. Do
we still notice them when
we walk by?

suffering. Why? Is it because we're cruel or because we're
kind? Does it say something good about us, or something
bad?

The woman who said, "Oh God, that poor child's family" was compassionate. But why did she pick that family
to feel sorry for? She had just heard about 10,000 people
dying in an earthquake. She had just heard about millions
starving to death in Ethiopia.

What is compassion, anyway? What is it *for*? What is
its place in our lives?

Melissa Morrison in New York:
Seeing suffering in the big city

Melissa Morrison works in a New York advertising agency. This is what she says when someone asks her about compassion:

"I grew up in a small town in Wisconsin. I went to college not far from there. When I moved to New York City it was quite a shock to me. My first day I saw a man collapsed on the sidewalk. I didn't know if he was drunk or sick. His clothes were dirty. He was covered with bruises. It was right in the heart of town. It was a cold winter day. It was below freezing.

"What shocked me wasn't how he looked — I'd seen sights like that before. What shocked me was what everybody else was doing. They were walking around him. They were *stepping over him*. No one was helping him. They were just ignoring it. They acted as if it were the most common sight in the world.

"So I went over to him, and I tried to wake him up. I'm not very strong. An older man stopped to help me. And a woman stopped and asked if she could help. We asked her to call an ambulance.

"And here's what I thought the moral was. First of all, people in the big city are hard-hearted. They're not very big in the compassion department. I don't know how they got that way. On the other hand, you can reach them. You just have to set an example. They saw me helping, then they stopped to help. Set an example and people will follow. That was the moral of that story, I thought then.

"That was five years ago. I've lived in New York City for five years now. Every day I move through crowds. I see hundreds, maybe thousands of people. Every day on the way to work I see somebody collapsed on the sidewalk, or in some other kind of trouble. If a homeless person asks me for some change I give him something. But if I see somebody collapsed on the street I walk right by. I can't be late to my job every day.

"I'm not so sure anymore what the moral of the story is."

What is compassion? Is it something everyone feels or something only a few of us feel? Do people have less of it than they used to? Is it a feeling we can't do much about anyway, nowadays, since it's the government's job to help the needy? Are our feelings of any use, then? Why should we feel compassionate? What do we get out of it? *Should* we get anything out of it?

People have always asked questions like these. In the pages that follow you'll find some of the answers they've come up with.

2

NO MAN IS AN ISLAND

JOHN DONNE LIVED about 400 years ago. He was a poet and a clergyman. Once he gave a sermon on the subject of church bells. In Donne's time the great bell in the church tower would be rung when somebody died. This was called a "death knell." When a bell tolled in those days and you asked, "Who is that for?" you were asking, "Who has died?"

Christian monks fed the poor. They believed that all people are connected and that we are responsible for each other.

13

This is part of Donne's sermon:
>No man is an island, entire of itself;
>every man is a piece of the Continent,
>a part of the maine; if a clod be washed
>away by the sea, Europe is the less...
>
>Any man's death diminishes me, because I
>am involved in *mankind.* And therefore
>never send to know for whom the bell tolls;
>it tolls for thee.

With this sermon Donne gave a definition of compassion. Compassion comes from our *connection* to other people. We're not separate, like islands. We're connected. Why does it matter to us what happens to other people? It matters because we feel connected to them.

Donne's idea doesn't only apply to death. Compassion in all things works because of a feeling of connection. When we don't feel compassion for someone in pain, it is because we don't feel connected.

Compassion is sharing another's feelings

No matter how cold-hearted the world may seem at times, *people do feel compassion.* It's one of the most common emotions people have. When a mother sees her

A mother and her child naturally share their feelings.

child scrape his knee, she drops whatever she's doing and rushes to help him. She feels that scrape as though it happened to her. When a friend tells you his bicycle was stolen, and you're really sorry, you're feeling compassion. You don't have to be as unhappy about your friend's loss as your friend is. You don't have to feel bad for more than a second. You're feeling compassion if you just wish for a moment that the bad thing didn't happen. Compassion is sharing someone else's feelings.

You may be in a movie theatre. There is a scene that

---

shows someone being tortured in a dentist's chair. You screw up your face. For a moment you're afraid for your teeth. You're afraid even though you know you're safe and no one is being tortured. It is only a movie, only actors pretending. That feeling of involvement is compassion, too. Compassion is what makes movies interesting. Compassion makes us feel connected even to imaginary people.

You see someone else suffering, *and you feel it too.* You may not feel everything the other person feels. But you do feel a little of what that person feels. You probably also feel the urge to help. No one knows exactly why people feel this way. They just do, sometimes.

If your friend's bike is stolen
and you feel bad, that is
compassion.

Young children will often get upset when another child is crying.

3

SCIENCE AND COMPASSION

Is compassion something you can be taught? Is it something you learn by example? Or are you born with it, like the ability to see and hear?

No doubt teaching and examples help. But research shows that we are born with the ability to feel compassion. How we feel it and what we do about it changes as we grow. We learn slowly to use our ability to feel compassion. But we learn to use it because we have a gift for it. We learn to use compassion the same way we learn to walk and talk. We see adults doing it and we learn by watching them.

Mental health workers study how children feel compassion. Here are some of the things they have learned: Newborn infants are upset when they hear other babies crying. No other sound upsets them as much. Older infants react to the pain of others as if it were happening to themselves. When they see another child get hurt and start to cry, they themselves begin to cry. Children around one year old begin to know the difference between someone else's pain and their own.

Chapter Three

Animals share many of the
feelings that humans
have.

In one case, a one-year-old boy saw a friend crying. He brought his mother over to comfort the friend, even though the friend's mother was also in the room. Slightly older children have a clearer idea of what other children need. In another case, a 15-month-old toddler named Michael saw his friend Paul crying. Michael fetched his teddy bear to comfort Paul. When that didn't work, Michael brought Paul's security blanket from another room.

By the time they are two or three years old, different children start to show different amounts of compassion.

Animals feel compassion

Even animals feel compassion. We can see it in the results of an experiment in which scientists tested the compassion of monkeys.

First, a group of monkeys were trained to avoid an electric shock. The monkeys would hear a sound. After the sound, they would be given an electric shock. The monkeys could avoid the shock by pulling a lever after they heard the sound. The monkeys learned to pull the lever so they would not get the shock.

Then the monkeys were separated. Only the first monkey could hear the sound. Only the second monkey could reach the lever. But they could see each other over a closed-circuit video. Whenever the first monkey heard the

---

sound it would become afraid. It knew a shock was coming, and it had no way of stopping it. The monkey who
could reach the lever could not hear the sound. But it
could see the expression of fear and shock on the other
monkey's face. The moment the first monkey showed that
it was afraid, the second monkey pulled the lever.

4

LEVELS OF COMPASSION

SOME PEOPLE HAVE NO COMPASSION AT ALL. Some have almost more than we can believe to be possible. Human compassion goes from point A to point Z. It goes from zero to an amount that cannot be measured.

Here is an extreme example of a lack of compassion:

In the early 1960s, the newspapers reported an ugly crime. A man planted a time bomb in his mother's luggage just before she got on a plane to Florida. He knew that if she died in a plane crash he would receive millions of dollars in insurance money.

The plane blew up in the air. His mother was killed—along with 40 other passengers.

Why does this man strike people as a monster? Was it because he killed his mother? Not really. When a son kills his mother we may call it an "unnatural" crime, because most people love their mothers. But we understand that there can also be hate between sons and mothers. It is a passionate relationship. A crime like that could be

During the 1972 Olympic Games, Arab terrorists took the Israeli team as hostages. They were eventually killed.

partly a crime of passion. The fact that he did it for money makes it worse, of course. The fact that he killed not one, but 40 people makes it even more horrible. But it is not just a question of numbers. The fact is that this man killed 40 strangers, without thinking at all about them or their families. This story tells us something about compassion. This, we can say, is the limit at one end. This is as little compassion as you can have.

The upper limits of compassion

What is the other limit? What is the most compassion a person can show for others?

A hand grenade falls into a group of soldiers. For a second it lays there without going off. There's no knowing how long it will be before it explodes. It could take another half a second, or another two seconds.

This has happened many times in combat.

Soldiers react differently in a situation like this. Some just stand there and can't move. If that happens, everyone nearby is killed by the explosion.

Most soldiers do what they have been trained to do: yell and lay flat on the ground. Everyone within range of

We are often made to feel uncomfortable by someone else's misfortune.

Military heroes often risk their own lives in order to save others.

the hand grenade is killed or injured by flying metal fragments called "shrapnel."

Some soldiers run. That doesn't do any good either. There isn't time to get away before the grenade goes off.

Some soldiers take a chance. They reach for the hand grenade and throw it back where it came from as fast as they can. Whether or not this works depends on how much time is left before the hand grenade goes off.

In some rare instances there is a soldier who, probably without even thinking, covers the grenade with his body. He gives his life to save the lives of his buddies. The government gives his family a medal in his name.

26

Where do we fit in?

Most of us are just as troubled by that soldier as we are by the man who put the time bomb in his mother's luggage. Maybe we're more troubled by the soldier. Because we know we are incapable of such self-sacrifice. We know we're better than the man who blew up the plane. But we strongly suspect we're not as good as the soldier. We don't know where he found the courage and compassion to give up his life to save the lives of his fellow soldiers. All we know is that people can be that brave and unselfish.

We feel that people who are so extraordinarily good are different from the rest of us. They are special. They do things we could never do.

But, in fact, these people are just human beings. They are just like the rest of us. So are the people we call mass murderers. They are all examples of how much—or how little—compassion a human being can feel and act on.

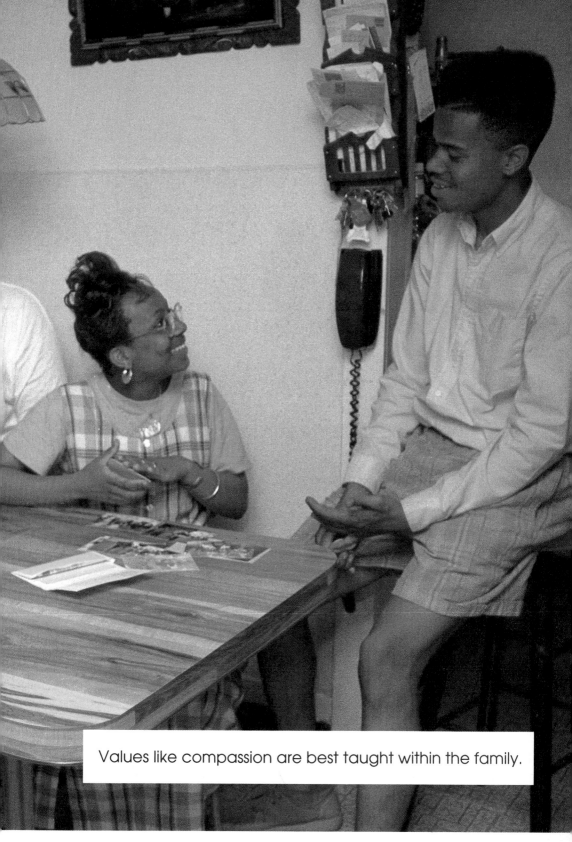

Values like compassion are best taught within the family.

All the major religions agree that compassion is a good thing.

5

COMPASSION IN THE GREAT RELIGIONS

ALL RELIGIONS PREACH COMPASSION in some form. There aren't any religions that say: "Don't help other people. Look out for yourself."

The great religions disagree about many things. They disagree about how the world was created. They disagree about the nature of God. They even disagree about the purpose of life. They disagree about why we should treat each other with compassion. They disagree about how we should show our compassion. But they all agree that compassion is a good thing.

What the believers have done in the name of their religions is another matter. If people lived up to what their religions preached, the world would look very different.

Most of the world's population belong to one of the major religions: Christianity, Judaism, Islam, Hinduism, Buddhism, or Confucianism.

(Above)

Jesus taught that one should "love your enemies." That is, to show compassion to everyone, even those opposed to you.

(At right)

Judaism teaches that you should behave to other people the way you would like to be treated. This means that we should be compassionate.

Christianity

Compassion was at the center of Jesus' teaching. Wherever he went he defended the weak and the oppressed. He took up the cause of society's outcasts. A woman was being punished for adultery (having sex with a man who was not her husband). At the time the punishment was death by stoning. Jesus said, "Let he who is without sin cast the first stone." He was preaching compassion to the hostile crowd.

Jesus set a difficult standard for compassion. He said, "Love your enemies," and "Judge not, lest ye be judged." He said, "Inasmuch as ye have done it unto one of the least of these my brethren, ye have done it unto me." He asked of his followers that each of them develop as much compassion for others as he, Jesus, had for all mankind.

Judaism

Rabbi Hillel was a famous Jewish teacher and scholar who lived before the time of Christ. Someone once challenged him: "I'll study with you if you can teach me the whole Law while I stand on one foot."

Rabbi Hillel said: "'Do not do to other people what you wouldn't want them to do to you.' All the rest is commentary. Go and learn it." That means that compassion is the foundation for all the teachings of Judaism. If a Jew is

Hindus believe that all life is connected. One must show compassion to all living things because even a fly may be carrying a human soul.

compassionate, he or she will obey all the laws of the Jewish faith. Jews must be compassionate to show their gratitude to God. Later, Jesus rephrased Rabbi Hillel's advice into what is now called "The Golden Rule." Jesus said: "Do unto others as you would have them do unto you."

Islam

Islam is the religion of the people we call Moslems or Muslims. It is most commonly practiced in the Mideast and in Africa. The Koran is the holy book of Islam. The

Moslems believe that one must give money to those less fortunate. This is the way to get to heaven.

Koran says that one of a Muslim's basic duties is to give alms, or money, to the poor. What reason does Islam give for the performing of this good work? Islam means "submission to God's will." Muslims, then, must be compassionate because it is God's will.

Hinduism

Hinduism is most commonly practiced in India. Hindus believe that God is present in everything. Most Hindus believe in reincarnation. That is, they believe that after you die you come back as something else. What you come back as depends on the kind of life you led before you died. If you live a bad, selfish life, you'll come back as an animal. If you live a good life, you will come back as a higher kind of person. So compassion is rewarded in Hinduism.

Hindus are often vegetarians. Some Hindu holy men literally will not hurt a fly; they wear gauze over their mouths in case an insect flies in and kills itself. Even an insect may carry a human soul. So all lives are equally precious.

For Hindus, compassion is based on the fact that people are all connected to each other. A Hindu is compassionate because of the oneness of all life.

Buddhism

Buddhism grew out of Hinduism. It is a religion of turning away from desire. Its central aim is to get rid of selfishness, because selfishness is the source of all suffering. Buddhists seek serenity. They would not want to feel compassion; they would not want to feel any strong emotion. But a good Buddhist behaves compassionately.

Just as Christians are supposed to follow Christ's example, Buddhists are supposed to follow Buddha's example. Compassion for mankind was the Buddha's reason for "turning back" after finding enlightenment. He did not allow himself to die, because he had to teach compassion to his fellow humans.

The way Buddha died showed both his compassion and his contempt for life. He was stopping at an inn. His host served him some porridge, unaware of the fact that the porridge was poisoned. The Buddha knew it was poisoned but he ate it anyway, rather than hurt his host's feelings. A stranger's feelings were more important to the Buddha than life itself.

Confucianism

Confucianism is the most widely practiced religion in China. Confucius helped to spread these teachings, but he did not invent them. Confucians seek oneness with

Buddhists practice to be "unselfish." By giving, rather than taking, they try to perfect themselves.

society and with nature. According to Confucianism, all men are good. One of the golden rules of Confucianism is expressed by the words: "What you do not wish done to yourself do not do to the other man." Doesn't this sound almost exactly like "The Golden Rule?"

Men and women have always valued compassion as an ideal. But they have seldom managed to live up to it. That is why we need the great religions and philosophies to preach it.

6

THE CASE AGAINST COMPASSION

MAYBE IT *DOESN'T* MEAN VERY MUCH that so many people say compassion is good. Maybe it is only that compassion is a safe thing to talk about. No one is afraid of a compassionate person. A compassionate person won't hurt you. So whether you are compassionate or not, it doesn't worry you when someone else says compassion is a good thing.

From time to time, however, there have actually been people who have come out against compassion. For example, in one of the books of the ancient Greek philosopher, Plato, a man is asked, "What is right?" And he answers: "Right is the interest of the strongest." There are certainly a lot more people who believe this than would say it. It is the principle that often guides treaties between governments. Many wars have been started by leaders who believed that "might makes right." For them, a strong country can demand things from other countries.

Nietzsche

Friedrich Nietzsche (nee-chee) was a German philosopher. One point he made over and over was that he did not believe in the teachings of Judaism and Christianity. He called it "slave morality." He thought of it as the weak many ganging up on the strong few. The most worthwhile things, Nietzsche argued, are the best things, the exceptional things. He admired great courage, great strength, great talent. According to Nietzsche, compassion is slave morality. It asks the strong to suffer for the weak.

Social Darwinsim

British scientist Charles Darwin showed that humankind comes from more primitive ancestors. This process is called "evolution." According to Darwin, and most scientists today, it works like this: plants, animals and human beings reproduce themselves. But every generation of every kind of living thing contains some differences from the individuals of the generation that went before. Some of these differences, or variations, are better suited to life than others. These variations, the "fittest" ones, survive and reproduce themselves. The "unfit" ones don't. In time, this process leads to new types of plants, animals and human beings. And some things "die out." They become extinct.

Charles Darwin's theories about "survival of the fittest" were applied to society's problems. Poor people, unable to get ahead, should be left alone to die out, like the dinosaurs. This was called "social Darwinism."

The unfit are weeded out

A British philosopher named Herbert Spencer applied Darwin's theory to morality and social life. Animals struggle for survival, said Spencer. Human beings struggle to better themselves and to live more comfortable lives. In both cases the result is an improvement. The unfit are weeded out; the best remain. Therefore, said Spencer, social programs to help the poor do harm rather than good. Such programs interfere with nature's plan.

Herbert Spencer died almost one hundred years ago. Today "Social Darwinism" is no longer taken seriously. But it is still talked about by some people, such as those who object to paying taxes for welfare programs.

The Third Man

People who can't feel compassion have a hard time understanding people who can. This isn't surprising, since compassion is based on the ability to understand how other people feel.

A movie called *The Third Man* is about a man who has an amazing lack of compassion. In the course of the movie, Rollo Martimes finds out that his old friend Harry Lime sells watered-down medicine. Because of Harry, hundreds of children have died from taking the useless pills.

In one scene, Rollo and Harry are on top of a ferris wheel in an amusement park. Rollo tells Harry he knows about the terrible thing he has done. He can't understand how Harry, who is so pleasant and likeable, could commit such a crime. Harry Lime points to the crowd below—all the people look small as bugs from up there. "Look at them. What are any of those dots down there to you?" he asks. "If one of them disappeared, would you really care? If I told you I would give you $50,000 if one of those dots vanished, wouldn't you take it?"

There is another side to compassion, but think about what the world would be like if none of us could see our fellow men as human beings like ourselves.

7

INDIFFERENCE

WHAT HAVE WE LEARNED?

Against compassion: Plato, Nietzsche, Herbert Spencer. In favor of compassion: Islam, Judaism, Christianity, Hinduism, Buddhism, Confucianism... and practically everybody else. Practically everybody is "for" compassion. There is even scientific proof that compassion is a natural part of being human. Religion preaches it from every pulpit.

Why, then, do we see so little of it when we look around us? Why do we feel so little of it when we look inside ourselves? Why are there so many people in

Both the Greek philosopher Plato(at left) and the German philosopher, Nietzsche (at right) believed the strong should rule the weak. They believed that compassion made slaves of strong people.

trouble who aren't being helped? Why do we give a quar-
ter to a beggar, and spend six dollars on a movie? Why is
compassion the exception instead of the rule? If we could
understand why, maybe we could start to change the way
things are.

If compassion is so wonderful, why isn't it more widely
practiced? Is it because people agree with Nietzsche or
Herbert Spencer or Harry Lime? No, most people are
actually shocked by such attitudes. Most people really are
bothered by another person's pain; that's why they look
away from it.

Most people aren't against compassion. They are in
favor of it. They would like to live in a world where
everyone was compassionate. Most people aren't cruel,
either. They are merely indifferent, most of the time.
How do they get that way?

Let's go back to the first chapter of this book. People
are watching the Six O'Clock News.

"An estimated 10,000 Mexico City residents died in an
earthquake yesterday..."

"Sally Anne Kelly, the 11-year-old reported missing...
raped and beaten to death...."

"....Ethiopian famine worst of the decade...."

"....Two homeless women froze to death...."

"Koko the chimp returns safe...."

We feel compassion for people, not numbers

It wasn't such an unusual news day. Reports of death and disaster are always a large part of the news. Some disaster stories are considered news because they are important as well as bad—the famine, for example, and the earthquake. If you don't know about them, you don't know what is happening in the world. But other stories aren't that important on a grand scale. They are news because they appeal to a basic human emotion. They appeal to our compassion: Sally Anne Kelly, the murdered 11-year-old. Even the story about the chimpanzee—for some people, especially the story about the chimpanzee.

If we watch this news program we'll probably feel sadder for Sally Anne Kelly than we will for the people in the famine or the earthquake. If you think about it, that doesn't make sense. Thousands and thousands of people died in those other stories and only one person died in the Sally Anne Kelly story. But compassion doesn't occur in the part of the brain that does arithmetic. We feel compassion for people, not for numbers. The fact that there's only one person in the Sally Anne Kelly story brings an important point home to us. *There was only one Sally Anne Kelly. There will never be another.* We forget that

We see so much tragic news on television that we become numb
and unable to experience feelings.

this is just as true of all those earthquake and famine
victims. Every one of them was just as important. But we
can't really understand that. It's too much for our minds
to grasp.

We feel compassion when we think we can help

All the stories in the news have one thing in common. You will not personally do anything about them. Oh, you could. You might. Some people do. You could help out at a shelter for the homeless. You could give money to relief foundations for famine victims or earthquake victims. You could write to Sally Anne's mother saying how sorry you are for her. But you are probably not going to do any of those things. You are certainly not going to do all of those things. It's too much. There is too much to be done. Most of us end up doing nothing.

Compassion feeds on action. We feel compassion most when we think we can help. It has to be that way. Otherwise we would be pulled in every direction by all the people who need help.

That is one reason people feel sorrier for individuals than for groups. That is an amount of compassion they can deal with. It makes some sense. They preserve their ability to feel compassion this way. The teenagers at the beginning of this book were joking about the chimp story. They were making fun of the news. But there are people who identify with the chimp story only. They identify with it because it's the only one that has a happy ending. There is at least one happy story in every newscast. That is because people who can't help need happy endings.

Remember the story in Chapter One about the small-town woman who came to live in New York. She started out feeling compassion and acting on it. But the demands became too much for her every day. She couldn't act on her compassion every day. So she lost the habit of compassion. She became numb. In her private life, she is probably still compassionate. She probably will always help a friend. But she has lost some of her ability to feel compassion toward strangers.

Is the same thing happening to all of us? On TV every day we see much more suffering than that woman sees on the street.

Compassion in modern times

People used to say that life was cheap in Asia because Asia was so crowded. No one knows if that was really true. But we do know that our country is getting more crowded every day. And the way we live gives us the feeling that we live in a very large community. Most people used to live in little towns where they knew everybody by name. People felt that they were one out of a hundred or a thousand. Nothing outside the town was very real to them. Nowadays, not only are the towns we live in much larger, but we feel more as if we live in the

whole world. Each of us is one out of *four billion* people.
All the people in the world!

Is the time we live in less compassionate than other
times? Questions like that are hard to answer. They always have mixed answers. In some ways yes; in some
ways no.

For a moment you might think, at least we are much
more compassionate to animals than people used to be.
We have the ASPCA, don't we? There are all kinds of laws
against cruelty to animals. Some people are trying to stop
the sale of fur coats. That would have been unheard of in
an earlier time. People did not used to consider the feelings of animals.

In the United States a hundred years ago, mobs of
people used to show up for hangings. In Europe a few
hundred years ago, criminals were publicly torn apart,
"drawn and quartered." Their heads were left to decay on
posts in the public square. It all seems barbaric to us
now. Yet when we are at war, our planes drop bombs on
innocent civilians. The pilots don't see the people being
crushed by falling buildings. They don't see the children
being burned alive. But it happens.

What is different about the way we react to other
people's pain today? It all has to do with seeing, doesn't
it? When possible, pain and suffering are kept out of

In wartime, pilots drop bombs on people. They often don't have to see the results.

sight. The mentally retarded, the crippled, the very old and feeble are shut up in hospitals. For many people the problem of the homeless is that they make our neighborhoods look ugly.

We see too much suffering that we can't do anything about. And we become indifferent. We *can* feel compassion, and we deliberately turn it off.

8

CRUELTY

INDIFFERENCE IS THE ABSENCE OF COMPASSION. Cruelty is the opposite of compassion. Cruelty can confuse us. It is bad enough when people cause pain in order to get their way. But why do people want to cause pain for its own sake?

The truth is that it is easy to explain why people are cruel. People aren't born evil, but they are born helpless. As they grow up they look for ways to be strong. When people don't feel strong, they become afraid. Cruelty is a way people have of feeling strong. After all, if you can hurt a person it usually means you're stronger than they are; otherwise, they would hurt you back.

Almost all of us are cruel sometimes. We may be in a bad mood. We haven't been getting our way. We are frustrated. We feel stupid. We feel helpless. Some completely innocent person asks us a question. We snap at them, or cut them down with a nasty remark. It feels good....while we're doing it, anyway. For a brief moment, we are hurting someone else. So we are not feeling our own hurt.

Teenagers often go through a cruel phase. They are struggling to break out of childhood. It is important for them to feel strong. So they do it at the expense of other people.

Some people are cruel all their lives. They gain the appearance of strength by giving pain and making other people feel helpless. But inside, they feel weak and hurt.

Compassion is a basic emotion that we are born with. It does not come from something else. Cruelty is not a basic emotion. It is a feeling that people can learn. But it is based on something that is probably more powerful than compassion. It is based on our instinct for survival. It is based on our fear and our desire for strength.

The School Outcast

Many who aren't cruel as individuals are cruel as members of groups.

You are on the school bus. It is the first day of class. There is one kid who is skinnier and smaller than the rest. His eyes are a little crossed. The way he moves is odd. It's delicate, like a bird. He wears a funny-looking sweater. He doesn't talk to anyone. He looks afraid. What in the world is he afraid of?

Very soon, a few of the children discover that this boy screams whenever you pinch him.

Many people who are compassionate and caring change when they are with others.

In any group, the weakest member is quickly identified.

So the kids pinch this boy every day, to hear him scream. It usually starts with name-calling and teasing. Then they move on to the pinching. The screaming goes on every day.

In this school bus there are five types of children.

1. The screamer who gets teased.

2. The ones who started the teasing.

3. The ones who wouldn't have thought of it, but go along with it to be part of the crowd.

4. The ones who watch but don't feel anything one way or the other.

5. The ones who feel bad about it but ignore it.

There is also the bus driver. He doesn't do much to stop the other kids. He doesn't want that screaming boy on his bus anyway. He likes normal, healthy, brave kids. Eventually the boy stops taking the bus.

Does this sound familiar? In every school there is always someone who gets picked on more than anyone else. It happens everywhere.

Each child has his own reason for joining in. But taken all together the group has a reason, too. The classmate they're picking on is weak in a way that makes them uncomfortable.

He is all the things they are terrified of being. And deep down, they have the feeling that it might be catching.

By joining together to pick on the odd one, children are telling themselves that the odd one, the weak one, is completely different from themselves. Weakness and suffering have nothing to do with them.

Calling unpleasant things by pleasant-sounding names

Think about insults. When you insult someone you challenge that person to prove that he or she is not what you said they were. People react to an insult as though what you were saying could come true. That is why they get angry at you. It is an insult to be called "idiot" or "wimp" because people are terrified of being idiots and wimps.

Some people think it is just the words that are insulting. Every fifteen years or so well-meaning people come up with words for "old" and "crippled" that will seem less insulting. "Don't say 'old,' say 'Senior Citizen,'" they told us. Now they tell us, "Don't say 'senior citizen.' Say 'golden ager.'" They used to tell us, "Don't say 'crippled,' say 'handicapped.'" Now they tell us, "Don't say 'handi-capped,' say 'challenged.'" Whatever you call them, these are things we don't want to be if we can help it.

So the names for these things become insults. Then so-cial workers and doctors invent new names. But eventu-ally the new name becomes an insult too. You can't change the way we think by changing a name. The prob-lem isn't the way we use words. The problem is our fear. If we were not afraid, we could afford to be kind.

Our fear of contagion

Selfishness is a force that works against compassion. Selfishness leads to indifference. The temptation to feel strong at the expense of others leads to cruelty. But the most powerful force that kills compassion is fear. The hurt and helpless are outsiders, or at least we would like to think of them that way. Just as we think, "There but for the grace of God go I," we think, "That kind of thing doesn't happen to people like me. That has nothing to do with me." That is how and why we make outcasts out of the very people who most deserve our compassion.

Plato, and Nietzsche, and Spencer, and Harry Lime in *The Third Man* all said the same thing—*That could never be me: I'm safe."* And John Donne and all the great religions say the opposite: *"That* is *me."*

9

CONCLUSION

IN THIS BOOK WE'VE TRIED TO SHOW many different ideas about compassion—why people feel it and why they don't, what it springs from and what it leads to, what kills it, and the place it has in people's lives.

Compassion is a natural part of a healthy, grown-up human being. In many of us, though, it lies dormant. It is in us, but we are not in touch with it. This is bad, because without it we are incomplete. No one can prove it is better to feel compassion than not to feel it. It may give you a greater freedom of action not to feel it. But life has less meaning if you don't feel things.

If everybody were compassionate, the world would be a better place. But even if everybody weren't any more compassionate than they are, and only you and I were more compassionate, *we* would be better off. Without compassion we can't really understand how other people feel. We can't feel a connection to other people. Without compassion, we can't love. So to be incapable of compassion is to be lonely.

How do we keep our compassion alive? That is a prob-
lem we must each solve for ourselves. It is something
you must work at your whole life.

No one can tell you how much you should give of
yourself for other people. But it is worth remembering
that objects of compassion are not only people who are
poor and strange and far away. Your friends and neigh-
bors and family members need your compassion, too. On
a bad day, other people's compassion can be a real help
to us. Compassion is not an emotion for special times in
life, it is part of every day we live.

Glossary: *Explaining New Words*

ASPCA American Society for the Prevention of Cruelty to Animals

barbaric cruel and uncivilized

black market the illegal sale of government-controlled goods; in times of crisis many different kinds of goods, including food and drugs, can be government controlled.

civilians people not associated with the military

clergyman religious official, for example a minister, priest or rabbi

closed-circuit video an arrangement of television equipment in which camera and "live" picture are in the same place

crime of passion a crime committed for emotional reasons

decapitate to behead, take off the head

dormant alive, but not functioning; for example, a volcano is called "dormant" when it hasn't erupted in years

disembowel to remove the intestines

elemental   basic, not made of smaller parts

penicillin   a life-saving antibiotic drug, first used during the Second World War

exceptional   not ordinary; better than average

extinct   no longer in existence; having "died out"

extraordinarily   in a way far beyond the average

incapable   not able to do something

indifference   not having any concern or feeling for someone or something

morality   ideas of right and wrong behavior

reincarnation   the idea that after people die they are reborn in another body

serenity   the experience of peace and calmness, the lack of strife

submission   obedience and meekness

suffering   being unhappy or in pain

toll   to ring, as a bell

For Further Reading

Bantam, Miles. *Animal Rights* (from the Survival series). New York: Franklin Watts Inc., 1987.

Ferrell, Frank, et. al. *Trevor's Place: The Story of the Boy Who Brings Hope to the Homeless*. New York: Harper & Row, 1985
This book tells how one boy turned his compassion for the homeless into a shelter to help them.

Frank, Anne. *Diary of a Young Girl*. New York: Modern Library, 1958. The actual diary of a 13-year-old Jewish girl in hiding from the Nazis during World War II.

Greene, Bette. *Summer of My German Soldier*. New York: Bantam Books, 1973. A girl befriends an escaped prisoner of war.

Greene, Graham. *The Third Man*. Winchester, MA: Faber & Faber, 1988. The novel on which the movie was based.

Keyes, Daniel. *Flowers For Algernon*. New York: Harcourt Brace Jovanovich, 1966. A friendship between a retarded man and a young boy teaches both about compassion.

Silverstein, Shel. *The Giving Tree*. New York: Harper & Row 1964. A fable about compassion and friendship, by the poet and illustrator.

INDEX

About the Author

Alice Margulies is the pen name of Philip Margulies. Mr. Margulies is a free-lance writer living in New York. He is the recipient of a fiction fellowship from the New York Foundation of the arts and has completed a book-length manual on child abuse.

Photo Credits and Acknowledgments

Cover photo: Charles Waldron
Pages 2,24,26,32(below),34-35,38,41,43,50, Wide World; p.8,10,17,18,25,28-29,30,46,53,54-55, Stephanie FitzGerald; p.13, Bettman; p.15,Stuart Rabinowitz; p.20, Animals,Animals; p.32 (top), Art Resource.

Design and Production: Blackbirch Graphics, Inc.